"This generation of Christians inhabit cultures that sometimes reject not only biblical revelation about reality, b Questions for Restless Minds series p faced by young Christians to some of ers and leaders. Along the way, this s generation to learn how to think biblically when they face questions in years to come that perhaps no one yet sees coming."

—Russell Moore,

public theologian, *Christianity Today*

"If you're hungry to go deeper in your faith, wrestle with hard questions, and are dissatisfied with the shallow content on your social media newsfeed, you'll really appreciate this series of thoughtful deep dives on critically important topics like faith, the Bible, friendship, sexuality, philosophy, and more. As you engage with some world-class Christian scholars, you'll be encouraged, equipped, challenged, and above all invited to love God more with your heart, soul, mind, and strength."

—Andy Kim,

multiethnic resource director, InterVarsity Christian Fellowship

How Do We Know God Exists?

Questions for Restless Minds

Questions for Restless Minds

QUESTIONS FOR RESTLESS MINDS

How Do We Know God Exists?

William Lane Craig

D. A. Carson,
Series Editor

LEXHAM PRESS

How Do We Know God Exists?
Questions for Restless Minds, edited by D. A. Carson

Copyright 2022 Christ on Campus Initiative

Lexham Press, 1313 Commercial St., Bellingham, WA 98225
LexhamPress.com

Print ISBN 9781683595274
Digital ISBN 9781683595281
Library of Congress Control Number 2021937706

Lexham Editorial: Todd Hains, Abigail Stocker, Jessi Strong, Mandi Newell
Cover Design: Brittany Schrock
Typesetting: Abigail Stocker

The Christ on Campus Initiative exists to inspire students on college and university campuses to think wisely, act with conviction, and become more Christlike by providing relevant and excellent evangelical resources on contemporary issues.

Visit christoncampuscci.org.

Contents

Series Preface

D. A. CARSON, SERIES EDITOR

THE ORIGIN OF this series of books lies with a group of faculty from Trinity Evangelical Divinity School (TEDS), under the leadership of Scott Manetsch. We wanted to address topics faced by today's undergraduates, especially those from Christian homes and churches.

If you are one such student, you already know what we have in mind. You know that most churches, however encouraging they may be, are not equipped to prepare you for what you will face when you enroll at university.

It's not as if you've never known any winsome atheists before going to college; it's not as if you've never thought about Islam, or the credibility of the New Testament documents, or the nature of friendship, or gender identity, or how the claims of Jesus sound too exclusive and rather narrow, or the nature of evil. But up until now you've probably thought about such things within the shielding cocoon of a community of faith.

Now you are at college, and the communities in which you are embedded often find Christian perspectives to be at best oddly quaint and old-fashioned, if not repulsive. To use the current jargon, it's easy to become socialized into a new community, a new world.

How shall you respond? You could, of course, withdraw a little: just buckle down and study computer science or Roman history (or whatever your subject is) and refuse to engage with others. Or you could throw over your Christian heritage as something that belongs to your immature years and buy into the cultural package that surrounds you. Or—and this is what we hope you will do—you could become better informed.

But how shall you go about this? On any disputed topic, you do not have the time, and probably not the interest, to bury yourself in a couple of dozen volumes written by experts for experts. And if you did, that would be on *one* topic—and there are scores of topics that will grab the attention of the inquisitive student. On the other hand, brief pamphlets with predictable answers couched in safe slogans will prove to be neither attractive nor convincing.

So we have adopted a middle course. We have written short books pitched at undergraduates who want arguments that are accessible and stimulating, but invariably courteous. The material is comprehensive enough that it has become an important resource for pastors and other campus leaders who devote their energies to work with students. Each book ends with a brief annotated bibliography and study questions, intended for readers who want to probe a little further.

Lexham Press is making this series available as attractive print books and in digital formats (ebook and Logos resource). We hope and pray you will find them helpful and convincing.

1

INTRODUCTION

I T'S PERHAPS SOMETHING of a surprise that almost none of the so-called New Atheists have anything to say about arguments for God's existence. Instead, they tend to focus on the social effects of religion and question whether religious belief is good for society. One might justifiably doubt that the social impact of an idea for good or ill is an adequate measure of its truth, especially when there are reasons being offered to think that the idea in question really is true. Darwinism, for example, has certainly had at least some negative social influences, but that's hardly grounds for thinking the theory to be false and simply ignoring the biological evidence in its favor.

Perhaps the New Atheists think that the traditional arguments for God's existence are now passé and so no longer need refutation. If so, they are naïve. Over the last generation there has been a revival of interest among professional philosophers, whose business it is to think about difficult metaphysical questions, in arguments for the existence of God. This resurgence of interest has not escaped the notice of even popular culture. In 1980 *Time* ran a major story entitled "Modernizing the Case for God," which described the movement among contemporary philosophers to refurbish the traditional arguments for God's existence. *Time* marveled,

> In a quiet revolution in thought and argument that hardly anybody could have foreseen only two decades ago, God is making a comeback. Most intriguingly, this is happening not among theologians or ordinary believers, but in the crisp intellectual circles of academic philosophers, where the consensus had long banished the Almighty from fruitful discourse.[1]

According to the article, the noted American philosopher Roderick Chisholm opined that the reason atheism was so influential in the previous generation is that the brightest philosophers were atheists; but today, he observes, many of the brightest philosophers are theists, using a tough-minded intellectualism in defense of that belief.

The New Atheists are blissfully ignorant of this ongoing revolution in Anglo-American philosophy.[2] They are generally out of touch with cutting-edge work in this field. About the only New Atheist to interact with arguments for God's existence is Richard Dawkins. In his book *The God Delusion*, which has become an international best-seller, Dawkins examines and offers refutations of many of the most important arguments for God.[3] He deserves credit for taking the arguments seriously. But are his refutations cogent? Has Dawkins dealt a fatal blow to the arguments?

Well, let's look at some of those arguments and see. But before we do, let's get clear what makes for a "good" argument. An argument is a series of statements (called premises) leading to a conclusion. A sound argument must meet two conditions: (1) it is logically valid (i.e., its conclusion follows from the premises by the rules of logic), and (2) its premises are true. If an argument is sound, then the truth of the conclusion follows necessarily from the premises. But to be a good argument, it's not enough that an argument be sound. We also need to have some *reason* to think that the premises are true. A logically valid argument that has, wholly unbeknownst to us, true premises isn't a good argument for the conclusion. The premises have to have some degree of justification or warrant for us in order for a sound argument to be a good one. But how much warrant? The premises surely don't need to be known to be true with certainty—we know almost nothing to be true with certainty!

Perhaps we should say that for an argument to be a good one the premises need to be probably true in light of the evidence. I think that's fair, though sometimes probabilities are difficult to quantify. Another way of putting this is that a good argument is a sound argument in which the premises are more plausible in light of the evidence than their opposites. You should compare the premise and its negation and believe whichever one is more plausibly true in light of the evidence. A good argument will be a sound argument whose premises are more plausible than their negations.

Given that definition, the question is this: Are there good arguments for God's existence? Has Dawkins in particular shown that the arguments for God are no good? In order to find out, let's look at five arguments for God's existence.

THE
COSMOLOGICAL
ARGUMENT

THE COSMOLOGICAL ARGUMENT comes in a variety of forms. Here's a simple version of the famous argument from contingency:

1. Everything that exists has an explanation of its existence, either in the necessity of its own nature or in an external cause.

2. If the universe has an explanation of its existence, that explanation is God.

3. The universe exists.

4. Therefore, the universe has an explanation of its existence (from 1, 3).

5. Therefore, the explanation of the universe's existence is God (from 2, 4).

Now this is a logically airtight argument. That is to say, if the premises are true, then the conclusion is unavoidable. It doesn't matter if we don't *like* the conclusion. It doesn't matter if we have *other* objections to God's existence. So long as we grant the three premises, we have to accept the conclusion. So the question is this: Which is more plausible—that those premises are true or that they are false?

PREMISE 1

Consider the first premise. According to premise 1, there are two kinds of things: things which exist necessarily and things which are produced by some external cause. Let me explain.

Things that exist necessarily exist by a necessity of their own nature. It's impossible for them not to exist. Many mathematicians think that numbers, sets, and other mathematical entities exist in this way. They're not caused to exist by something else; they just exist necessarily.

By contrast, things that are caused to exist by something else don't exist necessarily. They exist contingently. They exist because something else has produced them. Familiar physical objects like people, planets, and galaxies belong in this category.

So premise 1 asserts that everything that exists can be explained in one of these two ways. This claim, when you reflect on it, seems very plausibly true. Imagine that you're hiking through the woods and come across a translucent ball lying on the forest floor. You'd naturally wonder how it came to be there. If one of your hiking partners said to you, "Don't worry about it! There isn't any explanation of its existence!", you'd either think he was crazy or figure that he just wanted you to keep moving. No one would take seriously the suggestion that the ball existed there with literally *no explanation*.

Now suppose you increase the size of the ball in this story to the size of a car. That wouldn't do anything to satisfy or remove the demand for an explanation. Suppose it were the size of a house. Same problem. Suppose it were the size of a continent or a planet. Same problem. Suppose it were the size of the entire universe. Same problem. Merely increasing the size of the ball does nothing to affect the need of an explanation. Since any object could be substituted for the ball in this story, that gives grounds for thinking premise 1 to be true.

It might be said that while premise 1 is true of everything *in* the universe, it is not true *of* the universe itself. Everything in the universe has an explanation, but the universe itself has no explanation.

Such a response commits what has been aptly called "the taxicab fallacy." For as the nineteenth-century atheist philosopher Arthur Schopenhauer quipped, premise 1 can't be dismissed like a taxi once you've arrived at your desired destination! You can't say that everything has an explanation of its existence and then suddenly exempt the universe. It would be arbitrary to claim that the universe is the exception to the rule. (God is *not* an exception to premise 1; see page 16.) Our illustration of the ball in the woods shows that merely increasing the size of the object to be explained, even until it becomes the universe itself, does nothing to remove the need for some explanation of its existence.

One might try to *justify* making the universe an exception to premise 1. Some philosophers have claimed that it's *impossible* for the universe to have an explanation of its existence. For the explanation of the universe would have to be some prior state of affairs in which the universe did not yet exist. But that would be nothingness, and nothingness can't be the explanation of anything. So the universe must just exist inexplicably.

This line of reasoning is, however, obviously fallacious because it assumes that the universe is all there is, that if there were no universe there would be nothing. In other words, the objection assumes that atheism is true. The objector is thus begging the question in favor of atheism, arguing in a circle. The theist will agree that the explanation of the universe must be some (explanatorily) prior state of affairs in which the universe did not exist. But that state of affairs is God and his will, not nothingness.

So it seems that premise 1 is more plausibly true than false, which is all we need for a good argument.

PREMISE 2

What, then, about premise 2? Is it more plausibly true than false? Although premise 2 might appear at first to be controversial, what's really awkward for the atheist is that premise 2 is logically equivalent to the typical atheist response to the contingency argument. (Two statements are logically equivalent if it's impossible for one to be true and the other one false. They stand or fall together.) So what does the atheist almost always say in response to the contingency argument? He typically asserts the following:

A. If atheism is true, the universe has no explanation of its existence.

Since, on atheism, the universe is the ultimate reality, it just exists as a brute fact. But that is logically equivalent to saying this:

B. If the universe has an explanation of its existence, then atheism is not true.

So you can't affirm A. and deny B. But B. is virtually synonymous with premise 2! (Just compare them.) So by saying that, given atheism, the universe has no explanation, the atheist is implicitly admitting premise 2: if the universe does have an explanation, then God exists.

Besides that, premise 2 is very plausible in its own right. For think of what the universe is: *all* of space-time reality, including *all* matter and energy. It follows that if the universe has a cause of its existence, that cause must be a non-physical, immaterial being beyond space and time. Now there are only two sorts of things that could fit that description: either an abstract object like a number or else an unembodied mind. But abstract objects can't cause anything. That's part of what it means to be abstract. The number seven, for example, can't cause any effects. So if there is a cause of the universe, it must be a transcendent, unembodied mind, which is what Christians understand God to be.

PREMISE 3

Premise 3 is undeniable for any sincere seeker after truth. Obviously the universe exists!

CONCLUSION

From these three premises it follows that God exists. Now if God exists, the explanation of God's existence lies in the necessity of his own nature, since, as even the atheist recognizes, it's impossible for God to have a cause. So if this argument is successful, it proves the existence of a necessary, uncaused, timeless, spaceless, immaterial, personal creator of the universe. This is truly astonishing!

DAWKINS'S RESPONSE

So what does Dawkins have to say in response to this argument? Nothing! Just look at pages 77–78 of his book where you would expect this argument to come up. All you'll find is a brief discussion of some watered down versions of Thomas Aquinas's arguments, but nothing about the argument from contingency. This is quite remarkable, since the argument from contingency is one of the most famous arguments for God's existence and is defended today by philosophers such as Alexander Pruss, Timothy O'Connor, Stephen Davis, Robert Koons, and Richard Swinburne, to name a few.[4]

THE KALAM
COSMOLOGICAL
ARGUMENT

HERE'S A DIFFERENT version of the cosmological argument, which I have called the *kalam* cosmological argument in honor of its medieval Muslim proponents (*kalam* is the Arabic word for theology):

1. Everything that begins to exist has a cause.

2. The universe began to exist.

3. Therefore, the universe has a cause.

Once we reach the conclusion that the universe has a cause, we can then analyze what properties such a cause must have and assess its theological significance.

Now again the argument is logically ironclad. So the only question is whether the two premises are more plausibly true than their denials.

PREMISE 1

Premise 1 seems obviously true—at the least, more so than its negation. First, it's rooted in the necessary truth that something cannot come into being uncaused from nothing. To suggest that things could just pop into being uncaused out of nothing is literally worse than magic. Second, if things really could come into being uncaused out of nothing, then it's inexplicable why just anything and everything do not come into existence uncaused from nothing. Third, premise 1 is constantly confirmed in our experience as we see things that begin to exist being brought about by prior causes.

PREMISE 2

Premise 2 can be supported both by philosophical argument and by scientific evidence. The philosophical arguments aim to show that there cannot have been an infinite regress of past events. In other words, the series of past events must be finite and have had a beginning. Some of these arguments try to show that it is impossible for an actually infinite number of things to exist; therefore, an infinite number of past events cannot exist. Others try to show that an actually infinite series of past events could never elapse; since the series of past events has obviously elapsed, the number of past events must be finite.

The scientific evidence for premise 2 is based on the expansion of the universe and the thermodynamic properties of the universe. According to the Big Bang model of the origin of the universe, physical space and time, along with all the matter and energy in the universe, came into being at a point in the past about 13.7 billion years ago (Fig. 1).

What makes the Big Bang so amazing is that it represents the origin of the universe from literally nothing. As the physicist P. C. W. Davies explains, "the coming into being of the universe, as discussed in modern science ...

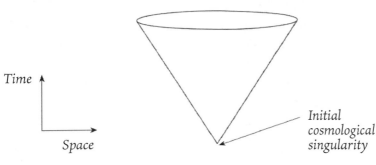

Figure 1: Geometrical Representation of Standard Model Space-Time. Space and time begin at the initial cosmological singularity, before which literally nothing exists.

is not just a matter of imposing some sort of organization ... upon a previous incoherent state, but literally the coming-into-being of all physical things from nothing."[5]

Of course, cosmologists have proposed alternative theories over the years to try to avoid this absolute beginning, but none of these theories has commended itself to the scientific community as more plausible than the Big Bang theory. In fact, in 2003 Arvind Borde, Alan Guth, and Alexander Vilenkin proved that *any* universe that is, on average, in a state of cosmic expansion cannot be eternal in the past but must have an absolute beginning. Their proof holds regardless of the physical description of the very early universe, which still eludes scientists, and applies even to any wider multiverse of which our universe might be thought to be a part. Vilenkin pulls no punches:

It is said that an argument is what convinces reasonable men and a proof is what it takes to convince even an unreasonable man. With the proof now in place, cosmologists can no longer hide behind the possibility of a past-eternal universe. There is no escape, they have to face the problem of a cosmic beginning.[6]

Moreover, in addition to the evidence based on the expansion of the universe, we have thermodynamic evidence for the beginning of the universe. The Second Law of Thermodynamics predicts that in a finite amount of time, the universe will grind down to a cold, dark, dilute, and lifeless state. But if it has already existed for infinite time, the universe should now be in such a desolate condition. Scientists have therefore concluded that the universe must have begun to exist a finite time ago and is now in the process of winding down.

CONCLUSION

It follows logically from the two premises that the universe has a cause. The prominent New Atheist philosopher Daniel Dennett agrees that the universe has a cause, but he thinks that the cause of the universe is itself! Yes, he's serious. In what he calls "the ultimate boot-strapping trick," he claims that the universe created itself.[7]

Dennett's view is plainly nonsense. Notice that he's not saying that the universe is self-caused in the sense that it has always existed. No, Dennett agrees that the universe had an absolute beginning but claims that the universe brought itself into being. But this is clearly impossible, for in order to create itself, the universe would have to already exist. It would have to exist before it existed! Dennett's view is thus logically incoherent. The cause of the universe must therefore be a transcendent cause beyond the universe.

So what properties must such a cause of the universe possess? As the cause of space and time, it must transcend space and time and therefore exist timelessly and non-spatially (at least without the universe). This transcendent cause must therefore be changeless and immaterial because (1) anything that is timeless must also be unchanging and (2) anything that is changeless must be non-physical and immaterial since material things are constantly changing at the molecular and atomic levels. Such a cause must be without a beginning and uncaused, at least in the sense of lacking any prior causal conditions, since there cannot be an infinite regress of causes. Ockham's Razor (the principle that states that we should not multiply causes beyond necessity) will shave away any other causes since only one cause is required to explain the effect. This entity must be unimaginably powerful, if not omnipotent, since it created the universe without any material cause.

Finally, and most remarkably, such a transcendent first cause is plausibly personal. We've already seen in our discussion of the argument from contingency that the personhood of the first cause of the universe is implied by its timelessness and immateriality. The only entities that can possess such properties are either minds or abstract objects like numbers. But abstract objects don't stand in causal relations. Therefore, the transcendent cause of the origin of the universe must be an unembodied mind.[8]

Moreover, the personhood of the first cause is also implied since the origin of an effect with a beginning is a cause without a beginning. We've seen that the beginning of the universe was the effect of a first cause. By the nature of the case, that cause cannot have a beginning of its existence or any prior cause. It just exists changelessly without beginning, and a finite time ago it brought the universe into existence. Now this is very peculiar. The cause is in some sense eternal and yet the effect that it produced is not eternal but began to exist a finite time ago. How can this happen? If the sufficient conditions for the effect are eternal, then why isn't the effect also eternal? How can a first event come to exist if the cause of that event exists changelessly and eternally? How can the cause exist without its effect?

There seems to be only one way out of this dilemma, and that's to say that the cause of the universe's beginning is a personal agent who freely chooses to create a universe in time. Philosophers call this type of causation "agent causation," and because the agent is free, he can initiate new effects by freely bringing about conditions that were not previously present. Thus, a finite time ago a creator could have freely brought the world into being at that moment. In this way, the creator could exist changelessly and eternally but choose to create the world in time.

(By "choose" one need not mean that the creator changes his mind about the decision to create, but that he freely and eternally intends to create a world with a beginning.) By exercising his causal power, he therefore brings it about that a world with a beginning comes to exist.[9] So the cause is eternal, but the effect is not. In this way, then, it is possible for the temporal universe to have come to exist from an eternal cause: through the free will of a personal creator.

So on the basis of an analysis of the argument's conclusion, we may therefore infer that a personal creator of the universe exists who is uncaused, without beginning, changeless, immaterial, timeless, spaceless, and unimaginably powerful.

On the contemporary scene, philosophers such as Stuart Hackett, David Oderberg, Mark Nowacki, and I have defended the *kalam* cosmological argument.[10]

DAWKINS'S RESPONSE

Now, fortunately, Dawkins does address this version of the cosmological argument. Remarkably, however, he doesn't dispute either premise of the argument! Instead, he questions the *theological significance* of the argument's conclusion. He complains,

Even if we allow the dubious luxury of arbitrarily conjuring up a terminator to an infinite regress and giving it a name, there is absolutely no reason to endow that terminator with any of the properties

27

normally ascribed to God: omnipotence, omni-science, goodness, creativity of design, to say noth-ing of such human attributes as listening to prayers, forgiving sins and reading innermost thoughts.[11]

Apart from the opening dig,[12] this is an amazingly con-cessionary statement. Dawkins doesn't deny that the argument successfully demonstrates the existence of an uncaused, beginningless, changeless, immaterial, timeless, spaceless, and unimaginably powerful, personal creator of the universe. He merely complains that this cause hasn't been shown to be omnipotent, omniscient, good, creative of design, listening to prayers, forgiving sins, and reading innermost thoughts. So what? The argument doesn't aspire to prove such things. It would be a bizarre form of atheism—indeed, one not worth the name—that conceded that there exists an uncaused, beginningless, changeless, immaterial, timeless, spaceless, and unimaginably powerful, personal creator of the universe, who *may*, for all we know, also pos-sess the further properties listed by Dawkins![13]

Dawkins does have a bit more to say about the *kalam* cosmological argument. He asserts, "It is more parsimo-nious to conjure up, say, a 'big bang singularity,' or some other physical concept as yet unknown. Calling it God is at best unhelpful and at worst perniciously misleading."[14] I take it that the objection here is that something else of a purely physical nature can be regarded as the cause of the universe reached in the argument's conclusion. But as we've seen, this objection won't work. For the initial singularity is just the beginning point of the universe. So our very question is why the singularity came into being. It would be a fundamental misunderstanding to think of the singularity as some sort of super-dense pellet that has been lying dormant from eternity and that blew up a finite time ago. Rather, according the Big Bang theory, the singularity is the point at which physical space and time themselves, along with all matter and energy, began to exist. So there can be no physical cause of any sort of the Big Bang singularity. So what brought the universe into being? The principle of parsimony (or Ockham's Razor) advises us not to multiply causes beyond necessity; but the principle of explanatory adequacy requires us to posit such causes as are necessary to explain the effect, otherwise we would never seek any causes for anything. We must therefore posit a transcendent cause that is beyond space and time and is therefore non-physical in nature. We needn't call the personal creator of the universe "God" if Dawkins finds this unhelpful or misleading; but the point remains that a being such as described above must exist.

4

THE MORAL ARGUMENT

A NUMBER OF ETHICISTS such as Robert Adams, William Alston, Mark Linville, Paul Copan, John Hare, Stephen Evans, and others have defended various moral arguments for God.[15] In order to understand the version of the moral argument which I've defended in my own work, it's necessary that we grasp a couple of important distinctions.

First, we should distinguish between moral *values* and *duties*. Values have to do with whether something is good or bad. Duties have to do with whether something is right or wrong. Now you might think at first that this is a distinction without a difference: "good" and "right" mean the same thing, and the same goes for "bad" and "wrong." But if you think about it, you can see that this isn't the case. Duty has to do with moral obligation, what you ought or ought not to do. But obviously you're not morally obligated to do something just because it would be good for you to do it. For example, it would be good for you to become a doctor, but you're not morally obligated to become a doctor. After all, it would also be good for you to become a firefighter or a homemaker or a diplomat, but you can't do them all. So there's a difference between good/bad and right/wrong. Good/bad has to do with something's *worth*, while right/wrong has to do with something's being *obligatory*.

Second, there's the distinction between being *objective* or *subjective*. By objective I mean "independent of people's opinions." By subjective I mean "dependent on people's opinions." So to say that there are objective moral values is to say that something is good or bad independent of whatever people think about it. Similarly, to say that we have objective moral duties is to say that certain actions are right or wrong for us regardless of what people think about it. So, for example, to say that the Holocaust was objectively wrong is to say that it was wrong even though the Nazis who carried it out thought that it was right, and it would still have been wrong even if the Nazis had won World War II and succeeded in exterminating or brainwashing everybody who disagreed with them so that everyone believed the Holocaust was right.

With those distinctions in mind, here's a simple moral argument for God's existence:

1. If God does not exist, objective moral values and duties do not exist.

2. Objective moral values and duties do exist.

3. Therefore, God exists.

PREMISES 1 AND 2

What makes this argument so compelling is not only that it is logically airtight but also that people generally believe both premises. In a pluralistic age, people are afraid of imposing their values on someone else. So premise 1 seems correct to them. Moral values and duties are not objective realities (that is, valid and binding independent of human opinion) but are merely subjective opinions ingrained into us by biological evolution and social conditioning.

At the same time, however, people do believe deeply that certain moral values and duties such as tolerance, open-mindedness, and love are objectively valid and binding. They think it's objectively *wrong* to impose your values on someone else! So they're deeply committed to premise 2 as well.

DAWKINS'S RESPONSE

In fact, Dawkins himself seems to be committed to both premises! With respect to premise 1, Dawkins informs us, "there is at bottom no design, no purpose, no evil, no good, nothing but pointless indifference. … We are machines for propagating DNA. … It is every living object's sole reason for being."[16] But although he says that there is no evil, no good, nothing but pointless indifference, the fact is that Dawkins is a stubborn moralist. He says that he was "mortified" to learn that Enron executive Jeff Skilling regards Dawkins's *The Selfish Gene* as his favorite book because of its perceived Social Darwinism.[17] He characterizes "Darwinian mistakes" like pity for someone unable to pay us back or sexual attraction to an infertile member of the opposite sex as "blessed, precious mistakes" and calls compassion and generosity "noble emotions."[18] He denounces the doctrine of original sin as "morally obnoxious."[19] He vigorously condemns such actions as the harassment and abuse of homosexuals, the religious indoctrination of children, the Incan practice of human sacrifice, and prizing cultural diversity over the interests of Amish children. He even goes so far as to offer his own amended Ten Commandments for guiding moral behavior, all the while marvelously oblivious to the contradiction with his ethical subjectivism![20]

In his survey of arguments for God's existence, Dawkins does touch on a sort of moral argument that he calls the Argument from Degree.[21] But it bears little resemblance to the argument presented here. We're not arguing from degrees of goodness to a greatest good, but from the objective reality of moral values and duties to their foundation in reality. It's hard to believe that all of Dawkins's heated moral denunciations and affirmations are really intended to be no more than his subjective opinion, as if to whisper with a wink, "Of course, I don't think that child abuse and homophobia and religious intolerance are *really* wrong! Do whatever you want—there's no moral difference!" But the affirmation of objective values and duties is incompatible with his atheism, for on naturalism we're just animals, relatively advanced primates, and animals are not moral agents. Affirming both of the premises of the moral argument, Dawkins is thus, on pain of irrationality, committed to the argument's conclusion, namely, that God exists.

THE EUTHYPHRO DILEMMA

Although Dawkins doesn't raise the following objection, one frequently hears it raised by nonbelievers in response to the moral argument. It's called the Euthyphro Dilemma, named after a character in one of Plato's dialogues. It basically goes like this: Is something good because God wills it? Or does God will something because it is good? If you say that something is good because God wills it, then what is good becomes arbitrary. God could have willed that hatred is good, and then we would have been morally obligated to hate one another. That seems crazy. Some moral values, at least, seem to be necessary. But if you say that God wills something because it is good, then what is good or bad is independent of God. In that case, moral values and duties exist independently of God, which contradicts premise 1.

The weakness of the Euthyphro Dilemma is that the dilemma it presents is a false one because there's a third alternative: namely, *God wills something because he is good*. God's own nature is the standard of goodness, and his commandments to us are expressions of his nature. In short, our moral duties are determined by the commands of a just and loving God.

So moral values are not independent of God because God's own character defines what is good. God is essentially compassionate, fair, kind, impartial, and so on. His nature is the moral standard determining good and bad. His commands necessarily reflect in turn his moral nature. Therefore, they are not arbitrary. The morally good/bad is determined by God's nature, and the morally right/wrong is determined by his will. God wills something because he is good, and something is right because God wills it.

This view of morality has been eloquently defended in our day by such well-known philosophers as Robert Adams, William Alston, and Philip Quinn. Yet atheists continue to attack the straw men erected by the Euthyphro Dilemma. In the recent *Cambridge Companion to Atheism* (2007), for example, the article on God and morality, written by a prominent ethicist, presents and criticizes only the view that God arbitrarily made up moral values—a straw man that virtually nobody defends. Atheists have to do better than that if they're to defeat contemporary moral arguments for God's existence.

5

THE
TELEOLOGICAL
ARGUMENT

W E NOW COME to the teleological argument, or the argument for design. Although advocates of the so-called Intelligent Design movement have continued the tradition of focusing on examples of design in biological systems, the cutting edge of the contemporary discussion concerns the remarkable fine-tuning of the cosmos for life.

Before we discuss this argument, it's important to understand that by fine-tuning one does *not* mean designed (otherwise the argument would be obviously circular). Rather during the last forty years or so, scientists have discovered that the existence of intelligent life depends upon a complex and delicate balance of initial conditions given in the Big Bang itself. This is known as the fine-tuning of the universe.

This fine-tuning is of two sorts. First, when the laws of nature are expressed as mathematical equations, you find appearing in them certain constants, like the constant that represents the force of gravity. These constants are *not* determined by the laws of nature. The laws of nature are consistent with a wide range of values for these constants. Second, in addition to these constants, there are certain arbitrary quantities that are put in just as initial conditions on which the laws of nature operate, for example, the amount of entropy or the balance between matter and anti-matter in the universe. Now all of these constants and quantities fall into an extraordinarily narrow range of life-permitting values. Were these constants or quantities to be altered by less than a hair's breadth, the life-permitting balance would be destroyed, and no living organisms of any kind could exist.[22]

For example, a change in the strength of the atomic weak force by only one part in 10^{100} would have prevented a life-permitting universe. The cosmological constant which drives the inflation of the universe and is responsible for the recently discovered acceleration of the universe's expansion is inexplicably fine-tuned to around one part in 10^{120}. Roger Penrose of Oxford University has calculated that the odds of the Big Bang's low entropy condition existing by chance are on the order of one out of $10^{10^{(123)}}$. Penrose comments, "I cannot even recall seeing anything else in physics whose accuracy is known to approach, even remotely, a figure like one part in $10^{10^{(123)}}$."[23] And it's not just *each* constant or quantity that must be exquisitely finely-tuned; their *ratios* to one another must be also finely-tuned. So improbability is multiplied by improbability by improbability until our minds are reeling in incomprehensible numbers.

So when scientists say that the universe is fine-tuned for life, they don't mean "designed"; rather they mean that small deviations from the actual values of the fundamental constants and quantities of nature would render the universe life-prohibiting or, alternatively, that the range of life-permitting values is incomprehensibly narrow in comparison with the range of assumable values. Dawkins himself, citing the work of the Astronomer Royal Sir Martin Rees, acknowledges that the universe does exhibit this extraordinary fine-tuning.

Here, then, is a simple formulation of a teleological argument based on fine-tuning:

1. The fine-tuning of the universe is due to either physical necessity, chance, or design.

2. It is not due to physical necessity or chance.

3. Therefore, it is due to design.

PREMISE 1

Premise 1 simply lists the three possibilities for explaining the presence of this amazing fine-tuning of the universe: physical necessity, chance, or design. The first alternative holds that there's some unknown Theory of Everything (TOE) that would explain the way the universe is. It *had* to be that way, and there was really no chance or little chance of the universe's not being life-permitting. By contrast, the second alternative states that the fine-tuning is due entirely to chance. It's just an accident that the universe is life-permitting, and we're the lucky beneficiaries. The third alternative rejects both of these accounts in favor of an intelligent Mind behind the cosmos, who designed the universe to permit life. The question is this: Which of these alternatives is the best explanation?

PREMISE 2

Premise 2 of the argument addresses that question. Consider the three alternatives. The first alternative, physical necessity, is extraordinarily implausible because, as we've seen, the constants and quantities are *independent* of the laws of nature. So, for example, the most promising candidate for a TOE to date, super-string theory or M-Theory, fails to predict uniquely our universe. String theory allows a "cosmic landscape" of around 10^{500} different possible universes governed by the present laws of nature, so it does nothing to render the observed values of the constants and quantities physically necessary. With respect to this first alternative, Dawkins notes that Sir Martin Rees rejects this explanation, and Dawkins says, "I think I agree."[24]

So what about the second alternative, that the fine-tuning of the universe is due to chance? The problem with this alternative is that the odds against the universe's being life-permitting are so incomprehensibly great that they can't be reasonably faced. Even though there will be a huge number of life-permitting universes lying within the cosmic landscape, nevertheless the number of life-permitting worlds will be unfathomably tiny compared to the entire landscape, so that the existence of a life-permitting universe is fantastically improbable. Students or laymen who blithely assert, "It could have happened by chance!" simply have no conception of the fantastic precision of the fine-tuning requisite for life. They would never embrace such a hypothesis in any other area of their lives—for example, in order to explain how there came to be a car in their driveway overnight.

DAWKINS'S DEFENSE OF CHANCE

In order to rescue the alternative of chance, its proponents have therefore been forced to adopt the hypothesis that there exists an infinite number of randomly ordered universes composing a sort of World Ensemble or multiverse of which our universe is but a part. Somewhere in this infinite World Ensemble, finely-tuned universes will appear by chance alone, and we happen to be in one such world. This is the explanation that Dawkins finds most plausible.[25]

IS A WORLD ENSEMBLE "UNPARSIMONIOUS"?

Now Dawkins is acutely sensitive to the charge that postulating a World Ensemble of randomly ordered universes seems to be, as he so nicely puts it, an "unparsimonious extravagance." But he retorts, "The multiverse may seem extravagant in sheer *number* of universes. But if each one of those universes is simple in its fundamental laws, we are still not postulating anything highly improbable."[26]

This response is confused on multiple levels. First, each universe in the ensemble is *not* simple but is characterized by a multiplicity of independent constants and quantities. If each universe were simple, then why did Dawkins feel the need to recur to the hypothesis of a World Ensemble in the first place? Besides, the issue is not the simplicity of the fundamental *laws*, for all the universes in the ensemble are characterized by the *same* laws—where they differ is in the values of the constants and quantities.

Second, Dawkins assumes that the simplicity of the whole is a function of the simplicity of the parts. This is an obvious mistake. A complex mosaic of a Roman face, for example, is made up of a great number of individually simple, monochromatic parts. In the same way, an ensemble of simple universes will still be complex if those universes vary in the values of their fundamental constants and quantities, rather than all sharing the same values.

Third, Ockham's Razor tells us not to multiply entities beyond necessity, so that the number of universes being postulated just to explain the fine-tuning of our universe is at face value extraordinarily extravagant. Appealing to a World Ensemble to explain the appearance of design is like using a sledge hammer to crack a peanut!

Fourth, Dawkins tries to minimize the extravagance of the postulate of a World Ensemble by claiming that despite its extravagant number of entities, still such a postulate is not highly improbable. It's not clear why this response is relevant or what this even means. For the objection under consideration is not that the postulate of a World Ensemble is improbable but that it is extravagant and unparsimonious. To say that the postulate isn't also highly improbable is to fail to address the objection. Indeed, it's hard to know what probability Dawkins is talking about here. He seems to mean the intrinsic probability of the postulate of a World Ensemble, considered apart from the evidence of fine-tuning. But how is such a probability to be determined? By simplicity? But then the problem is that Dawkins hasn't shown the World Ensemble hypothesis to be simple.

DAWKINS'S SUGGESTED MECHANISMS FOR GENERATING A WORLD ENSEMBLE

What Dawkins needs to say, it seems to me, is that the postulate of a World Ensemble may still be simple *if* there is a simple mechanism that through a repetitive process generates the many worlds. In that way the huge number of entities postulated isn't a deficit of the theory because the entities all issue from a very simple fundamental mechanism.

An Oscillating Model of the Universe

So what mechanisms does Dawkins suggest for generating such an infinite, randomly ordered World Ensemble? First, he suggests an oscillating model of the universe, according to which

> our time and space did indeed begin in our big bang, but this was just the latest in a long series of big bangs, each one initiated by the big crunch that terminated the previous universe in the series. Nobody understands what goes on in singularities such as the big bang, so it is conceivable that the laws and constants are reset to new values, each time. If bang-expansion-contraction-crunch cycles have been going on forever like a cosmic accordion, we have a serial, rather than parallel, version of the multiverse.[27]

49

Dawkins is apparently unaware of the many difficulties of oscillatory models of the universe that have made contemporary cosmologists skeptical of them. Back in the 1960s and 1970s, some theorists proposed oscillating models of the universe in an attempt to avert the initial singularity predicted by the Standard Model. The prospects of such models were severely dimmed in 1970, however, by Roger Penrose and Stephen Hawking's formulation of the singularity theorems that bear their names. The theorems disclosed that under very generalized conditions an initial cosmological singularity is inevitable. Since it's impossible to extend space-time through a singularity to a prior state, the Hawking-Penrose singularity theorems implied the absolute beginning of the universe. Reflecting on the impact of this discovery, Hawking notes that the Hawking-Penrose singularity theorems "led to the abandonment of attempts (mainly by the Russians) to argue that there was a previous contracting phase and a non-singular bounce into expansion. Instead almost everyone now believes that the universe, and time itself, had a beginning at the big bang."[28] Dawkins apparently labors under the delusion that a singularity does not form a boundary to space and time.

Moreover, the evidence of observational astronomy has been consistently against the hypothesis that the universe will someday recontract into a big crunch. Attempts to discover the mass density sufficient to generate the gravitational attraction required to halt and reverse the expansion continually came up short. In fact, recent observations of distant supernovae indicate that—far from slowing down—the cosmic expansion is actually accelerating! There's some sort of mysterious "dark energy" in the form of either a variable energy field (called "quintessence") or, more probably, a positive cosmological constant or vacuum energy that causes the expansion to proceed more rapidly. If the dark energy does indicate the existence of a positive cosmological constant (as the evidence increasingly suggests), then the universe will expand forever. According to the NASA website of the Wilkinson Microwave Anisotropy Probe, "For the theory that fits our data, the Universe will expand forever."[29]

Furthermore, wholly apart from the physical and observational difficulties confronting oscillatory models, the thermodynamic properties of such models imply the very beginning of the universe that their proponents sought to avoid. For entropy is conserved from cycle to cycle in such models, which has the effect of generating larger and longer oscillations with each successive cycle. As one scientific team explains, "The effect of entropy production will be to enlarge the cosmic scale, from cycle to cycle. ... Thus, looking back in time, each cycle generated less entropy, had a smaller cycle time, and had a smaller cycle expansion factor than the cycle that followed it."[30] Thus, as one traces the oscillations back in time, they become progressively smaller until one reaches a first and smallest oscillation. Zeldovich and Novikov therefore conclude, "The multicycle model has an infinite future, but only a finite past."[31] In fact, astronomer Joseph Silk estimates on the basis of current entropy levels that the universe cannot have gone through more than 100 previous oscillations.[32] This is far from sufficient to generate the sort of serial World Ensemble imagined by Dawkins.

Finally, even if the universe could oscillate from eternity past, such a universe would require an infinitely precise fine-tuning of initial conditions in order to persist through an infinite number of successive bounces. Thus, the mechanism Dawkins envisions for generating his many worlds is not simple but just the opposite. Moreover, such a universe involves a fine-tuning of a very bizarre sort since the initial conditions have to be set at minus infinity in the past. But how could that be done if there was no beginning?

Looking back on the discussion of oscillating models of the universe, quantum cosmologist Christopher Isham muses,

> Perhaps the best argument in favor of the thesis that the Big Bang supports theism is the obvious unease with which it is greeted by some atheist physicists. At times this has led to scientific ideas, such as continuous creation or an oscillating universe, being advanced with a tenacity which so exceeds their intrinsic worth that one can only suspect the operation of psychological forces lying very much deeper than the usual academic desire of a theorist to support his/her theory.[33]

In Dawkins's case, it is not hard to discern those psychological forces at work.

Lee Smolin's Evolutionary Cosmology

Dawkins's second suggested mechanism for generating a World Ensemble is Lee Smolin's evolutionary cosmology. Smolin imagines a scenario, Dawkins explains, according to which

> daughter universes are born of parent universes, not in a fully fledged big crunch, but more locally in black holes. Smolin adds a form of heredity: The fundamental constants of a daughter universe are slightly "mutated" versions of the constants of its parent. ... Those universes which have what it takes to "survive" and "reproduce" come to predominate in the multiverse. "What it takes" includes lasting long enough to "reproduce." Because the act of reproduction takes place in black holes, successful universes must have what it takes to make black holes. This ability entails various other properties. For example, the tendency of matter to condense into clouds and then stars is a prerequisite for making black holes. Stars also ... are the precursors to the development of interesting chemistry, and hence life. So, Smolin suggests, there has been a Darwinian natural selection of universes in the multiverse, directly favouring the evolution of black hole fecundity and indirectly favouring the production of life.[34]

Dawkins acknowledges that "not all physicists" are enthusiastic about Smolin's scenario. Talk about an understatement! For Smolin's scenario, wholly apart from its *ad hoc* and even disconfirmed conjectures, encounters insuperable difficulties.

First, a fatal flaw in Smolin's scenario is his assumption that universes fine-tuned for black-hole production would also be fine-tuned for the production of stable stars. In fact, the exact opposite is true: the most proficient producers of black holes would be universes that generate primordial black holes *prior* to star formation, so that life-permitting universes would actually be *weeded out* by Smolin's cosmic evolutionary scenario. Thus, it turns out that Smolin's scenario would actually make the existence of a life-permitting universe even more improbable.

Second, speculations about the universe's begetting "baby universes" via black holes have been shown to contradict quantum physics. The conjecture that black holes may be portals of wormholes through which bubbles of false vacuum energy can tunnel to spawn new expanding baby universes was the subject of a bet between Stephen Hawking and John Preskill, which Hawking in 2004 finally admitted, in an event much publicized in the press, that he had lost.[35] The conjecture would require that information locked up in a black hole could be utterly lost forever by escaping to another universe. One of the last holdouts, Hawking finally came to agree that quantum theory requires that information is preserved in black hole formation and evaporation. The implications? "There is no baby universe branching off, as I once thought. The information remains firmly in our universe. I'm sorry to disappoint science fiction fans, but if information is preserved, there is no possibility of using black holes to travel to other universes."[36] That means that Smolin's scenario is physically impossible.

These are the only mechanisms Dawkins suggests for generating a World Ensemble of randomly ordered universes. Neither of them is even tenable, much less simple. Dawkins has therefore failed to turn back the objection that his postulation of a randomly ordered World Ensemble is an unparsimonious extravagance.

FURTHER OBJECTIONS TO THE WORLD ENSEMBLE HYPOTHESIS

But there are even more formidable objections to the postulate of a World Ensemble of which Dawkins is apparently unaware. First, there's no independent evidence that a World Ensemble exists, much less one that is randomly ordered and infinite. Recall that Borde, Guth, and Vilenkin proved that any universe in a state of overall cosmic expansion cannot be infinite in the past. Their theorem applies to the multiverse, too. Therefore, since the multiverse's past is finite, only a finite number of other worlds may have been generated by now, so there's no guarantee that a finely-tuned world will have appeared in the ensemble. By contrast we do have independent evidence for the existence of a Cosmic Designer, namely, the other arguments for God's existence which we have been discussing. Thus, theism is, all else being equal, the better explanation.

Second, if our universe is just a random member of an infinite World Ensemble, then it's overwhelmingly more probable that we should be observing a much different universe than what we in fact observe. Roger Penrose has pressed this objection forcefully.[37] He calculates that it is inconceivably more probable that our solar system should suddenly form by the random collision of particles than that a finely-tuned universe should exist. (Penrose calls it "utter chicken feed" by comparison.) So if our universe were just a random member of a World Ensemble, it is incalculably more probable that we should be observing an orderly universe no larger than our solar system. Or again, if our universe were just a random member of a World Ensemble, then we ought to be observing highly extraordinary events, like horses' popping into and out of existence by random collisions, or perpetual motion machines, since such things are vastly more probable than all of nature's constants, and quantities' falling by chance into the virtually infinitesimal life-permitting range. Observable universes like those are simply much more plenteous in the World Ensemble than worlds like ours and, therefore, ought to be observed by us. We do not have such observations, which strongly disconfirms the multiverse hypothesis. On atheism, at least, it is therefore highly probable that there is no World Ensemble.

CONCLUSION

The fine-tuning of the universe is therefore plausibly due neither to physical necessity nor to chance. It follows that the fine-tuning is therefore due to design *unless* the design hypothesis can be shown to be even more implausible than its competitors.

DAWKINS'S CRITIQUE OF DESIGN

Dawkins contends the alternative of design is, indeed, inferior to the Many Worlds hypothesis. Summarizing what he calls "the central argument of my book," Dawkins argues,

1. One of the greatest challenges to the human intellect, over the centuries, has been to explain how the complex, improbable appearance of design in the universe arises.

2. The natural temptation is to attribute the appearance of design to actual design itself. …

3. The temptation is a false one, because the designer hypothesis immediately raises the larger problem of who designed the designer. …

4. The most ingenious and powerful crane [i.e., explanation] so far discovered is Darwinian evolution by natural selection. …

5. We don't have an equivalent explanation for physics. …

6. We should not give up hope of a better crane arising in physics, something as powerful as Darwinism is for biology. ...

[Therefore] God almost certainly does not exist.[38]

This argument is jarring because the atheistic conclusion, "Therefore, God almost certainly does not exist" doesn't follow from the six previous statements even if we concede that each of them is true and justified. At most, all that follows is that we should not infer God's existence on the basis of the appearance of design in the universe. But that conclusion is quite compatible with God's existence and even with our justifiably believing in God's existence on other grounds. Rejecting design arguments for God's existence does nothing to prove that God does not exist or even that belief in God is unjustified.

In any case, does Dawkins's argument succeed even in undermining the alternative of design? Step 5 alludes to the cosmic fine-tuning that has been the focus of our discussion. Dawkins holds out hope that "Some kind of multiverse theory could in principle do for physics the same explanatory work as Darwinism does for biology."[39] But he admits that we don't have it yet, nor does he deal with the formidable problems facing such an explanation of cosmic fine-tuning. Therefore, the hope expressed in step 6 represents nothing more than the faith of a naturalist. Dawkins insists that even in the absence of a "strongly satisfying" explanation for the fine-tuning in physics, still the "relatively weak" explanations we have at present are "self-evidently better than the self-defeating ... hypothesis of an intelligent designer."[40] Really? What is this powerful objection to the design hypothesis that renders it self-evidently inferior to the admittedly weak Many Worlds hypothesis?

The answer is contained in step 3. Dawkins's objection here is that we're not justified in inferring design as the best explanation of the complex order of the universe because then a new problem arises: who designed the Designer? (Because Dawkins erroneously thinks that the World Ensemble is simple, it never occurs to him to ask, "Who designed the World Ensemble?") This question is apparently supposed to be so crushing that it outweighs all the problems with the World Ensemble hypothesis.

Dawkins's objection, however, has no weight for at least two reasons. First, in order to recognize an explanation as the best, you don't need to have an explanation of the explanation. This is an elementary point in the philosophy of science. If archaeologists digging in the earth were to discover things looking like arrowheads and pottery shards, they would be justified in inferring that these artifacts are not the chance result of sedimentation and metamorphosis, but products of some unknown group of people, even though they had no explanation of who these people were or where they came from. Similarly, if astronauts were to come upon a pile of machinery on the back side of the moon, they would be justified in inferring that it was the product of intelligent agents, even if they had no idea whatsoever who these agents were or how they got there.

To repeat: in order to recognize an explanation as the best, you don't need to be able to explain the explanation. In fact, such a requirement would lead to an infinite regress of explanations so that nothing could ever be explained and science would be destroyed! For before any explanation could be acceptable, you'd need an explanation of it, and then an explanation of the explanation of the explanation, etc. Nothing could ever be explained.

So in the case at hand, in order to recognize that intelligent design is the best explanation of the appearance of design in the universe, one needn't be able to explain the Designer. Whether the Designer has an explanation can simply be left an open question for future inquiry.

Second, Dawkins thinks that in the case of a divine Designer of the universe, the Designer is just as complex as the thing to be explained, so that no explanatory advance is made. This objection raises all sorts of questions about the role played by simplicity in assessing competing explanations. First, Dawkins seems to confuse the simplicity of a hypothesis with the simplicity of the entity described in the hypothesis.[41] Positing a complex cause to explain some effect can be a very simple hypothesis, especially when contrasted with rival hypotheses. Think, for example, of our archaeologists' postulating a human fabricator to explain the arrowheads they discovered. A human being is a vastly more complex entity than an arrowhead, but the hypothesis of a human designer is a very simple explanation. It is certainly more simple than the hypothesis that the artifacts were the unintended result of, say, a stampede of buffalo that chipped a rock to look like an arrowhead. The point is that rival hypotheses are assessed by the criterion of simplicity, not the entities they postulate.

Second, there are many other factors besides simplicity that scientists weigh in determining which hypothesis is the best, such as explanatory power, explanatory scope, and so forth. A hypothesis that has, for example, broader explanatory scope may be less simple than a rival hypothesis but still be preferred because it explains more things. Simplicity is not the only, or even most important, criterion for assessing theories!

But leave all those problems aside. For Dawkins is plainly mistaken anyway in his assumption that a divine Designer is just as complex an entity as the universe. As a pure mind or consciousness without a body, God is a remarkably simple entity. A mind (or soul) is not a physical object composed of parts. In contrast to the contingent and variegated universe with all its inexplicable constants and quantities, a divine mind is amazingly simple. Dawkins protests, "A God capable of continuously monitoring and controlling the individual status of every particle in the universe *cannot* be simple."[42] This is just confused. Certainly a mind may have complex *ideas* (it may be thinking, for example, of the infinitesimal calculus) and may be capable of doing complex *tasks* (such as controlling the trajectory of every particle in the universe), but the mind *itself* is a remarkably simple, non-physical entity. Dawkins has evidently confused a mind's ideas and effects, which may, indeed, be complex, with a mind itself, which is an incredibly simple entity. Therefore, postulating a divine mind behind the universe most definitely does represent an advance in simplicity, for whatever that's worth.

In his book Dawkins triumphantly relates how he once presented his supposedly crushing argument at a Templeton Foundation conference on science and religion at Cambridge University, only to be rebuffed by the other participants, who told him that theologians have always held that God is simple.[43] They were quite right. Indeed, Dawkins's smug and self-congratulatory attitude about his misguided objection, sustained even in the face of repeated correction by prominent philosophers and theologians like Richard Swinburne and Keith Ward, is a wonder to behold.

Therefore, of the three alternatives before us—physical necessity, chance, or design—the most plausible of the three as an explanation of cosmic fine-tuning is design. The teleological argument thus remains as robust today as ever, defended in various forms by philosophers and scientists such as Robin Collins, John Leslie, Paul Davies, William Dembski, Michael Denton, and others.[44]

THE
ONTOLOGICAL
ARGUMENT

THE LAST ARGUMENT I wish to discuss is the famous ontological argument, originally discovered by St. Anselm. This argument has been reformulated and defended by Alvin Plantinga, Robert Maydole, Brian Leftow, and others.[45] I'll present the version of the argument as stated by Plantinga, one of its most respected contemporary proponents.

Plantinga's version is formulated in terms of possible worlds semantics. For those who are unfamiliar with the semantics of possible worlds, let me explain that by "a possible world" I do not mean a planet or even a universe, but rather a complete description of reality, or a way reality might be. Perhaps the best way to think of a possible world is as a huge conjunction p & q & r & s ... , whose individual conjuncts are the propositions $p, q, r, s, ...$. A possible world is a conjunction that comprises every proposition or its contradictory, so that it yields a complete description of reality—nothing is left out of such a description. By negating different conjuncts in a complete description we arrive at different possible worlds:

W_1: p & q & r & s ...

W_2: p & not-q & r & not-s ...

W_3: not-p & not-q & r & s ...

W_4: p & q & not-r & s ...

Etc.

Only one of these descriptions will be composed entirely of true propositions and so will be the way reality actually is, that is to say, the actual world.

Since we're talking about possible worlds, the various conjuncts that a possible world comprises must be capable of being true both individually and together. For example, the proposition "The Prime Minister is a prime number" is not even possibly true, for numbers are abstract objects that could not conceivably be identical with a concrete object like the Prime Minister. Therefore, no possible world will have that proposition as one of its conjuncts; rather its negation will be a conjunct of every possible world. Such a proposition is necessarily false, that is to say, it is false in every possible world. By contrast, the proposition "George McGovern is the President of the United States" is false in the actual world but could be true and so is a conjunct of some possible worlds. To say that George McGovern is the President of the United States in some possible world is to say that there is a possible complete description of reality having the relevant proposition as one of its conjuncts.

Similarly, to say that God exists in some possible world is to say that the proposition "God exists" is true in some complete description of reality.

Now in his version of the argument, Plantinga conceives of God as a being that is "maximally excellent" in every possible world. Plantinga takes maximal excellence to include such properties as omniscience, omnipotence, and moral perfection. A being that has maximal excellence in every possible world would have what Plantinga calls "maximal greatness." Now Plantinga argues,

1. It is possible that a maximally great being exists.

2. If it is possible that a maximally great being exists, then a maximally great being exists in some possible world.

3. If a maximally great being exists in some possible world, then it exists in every possible world.

4. If a maximally great being exists in every possible world, then it exists in the actual world.

5. If a maximally great being exists in the actual world, then a maximally great being exists.

6. Therefore, a maximally great being exists.

PREMISE 1

It might surprise you to learn that steps 2–6 of this argument are relatively uncontroversial. Most philosophers would agree that if God's existence is even possible, then he must exist. The principal issue to be settled with respect to Plantinga's ontological argument is what warrant exists for thinking the key premise "It is possible that a maximally great being exists" to be true.

The idea of a maximally great being is intuitively a coherent idea, and so it seems plausible that such a being could exist. In order for the ontological argument to fail, the concept of a maximally great being must be incoherent, like the concept of a married bachelor. The concept of a married bachelor is not a *strictly* self-contradictory concept (as is the concept of a married unmarried man), and yet it is obvious, once one understands the meaning of the words "married" and "bachelor," that nothing corresponding to that concept can exist. By contrast, the concept of a maximally great being doesn't seem even remotely incoherent. This provides some *prima facie* warrant for thinking that it is possible that a maximally great being exists.

DAWKINS'S RESPONSE

Dawkins devotes six full pages, brimming with ridicule and invective, to the ontological argument, without raising any serious objection to Plantinga's argument. He notes in passing Immanuel Kant's objection that existence is not a perfection; but since Plantinga's argument doesn't presuppose that it is, we can leave that irrelevance aside. He reiterates a parody of the argument designed to show that God does not exist because a God "who created everything while not existing" is greater than one who exists and creates everything.[46] Ironically, this parody, far from undermining the ontological argument, actually reinforces it. For a being who creates everything while not existing is a logical incoherence and is therefore impossible: there is no possible world that includes a non-existent being that creates the world. If the atheist is to maintain—as he must—that God's existence is impossible, the concept of God would have to be similarly incoherent. But it's not. That supports the plausibility of premise 1.

Dawkins also chortles, "I've forgotten the details, but I once piqued a gathering of theologians and philosophers by adapting the ontological argument to prove that pigs can fly. They felt the need to resort to Modal Logic to prove that I was wrong."[47] This is just embarrassing. The ontological argument just *is* an exercise in modal logic—the logic of the possible and the necessary. I can just imagine Dawkins making a spectacle of himself at this professional conference with his spurious parody, just as he similarly embarrassed himself at the Templeton Foundation conference in Cambridge with his flyweight objection to the teleological argument!

CONCLUSION

W E'VE EXAMINED FIVE traditional arguments for the existence of God in light of modern philosophy, science, and mathematics:

1. The cosmological argument from contingency

2. The *kalam* cosmological argument based on the beginning of the universe

3. The moral argument based upon objective moral values and duties

4. The teleological argument from fine-tuning

5. The ontological argument from the possibility of God's existence to his actuality

These are, I believe, good arguments for God's existence. That is to say, they are logically valid; their premises are true; and their premises are more plausible in light of the evidence than their negations. Therefore, insofar as we are rational people, we should embrace their conclusions. Much more remains to be said and has been said.[48] I refer you to the works cited in the footnotes and bibliography, should you wish to explore further. But I trust that enough has been said here to show that the traditional theistic arguments remain unscathed by the objections raised by the likes of New Atheists such as Richard Dawkins.

Acknowledgments

T HE SERIES Questions for Restless Minds is produced by the Christ on Campus Initiative, under the stewardship of the editorial board of D. A. Carson (senior editor), Douglas Sweeney, Graham Cole, Dana Harris, Thomas McCall, Geoffrey Fulkerson, and Scott Manetsch. The editorial board recognizes with gratitude the many outstanding evangelical authors who have contributed to this series, as well as the sponsorship of Trinity Evangelical Divinity School (Deerfield, Illinois), and the financial support of the MAC Foundation and the Carl F. H. Henry Center for Theological Understanding. The editors also wish to thank Christopher Gow, who created the study questions accompanying each book, and Todd Hains, our editor at Lexham Press. May God alone receive the glory for this endeavor!

Study Guide Questions

1. How familiar are you/what experience do you have with the New Atheists?

2. What is the taxicab fallacy?

3. Discuss questions that you have about each argument. Do they all make sense?

4. What is the difference between moral values and duties?

5. Which argument do you find the most compelling?

6. Which objections/counterarguments do you find most effective?

7. Do these discussions strengthen your faith? Why or why not?

8. What is the basis for your belief in God? If someone asked you why you believe in God, what would you say?

9. Spend some time reflecting on the reality of God's existence. Pray that God would make himself more real and present to you today and this week.

For Further Reading

THE COSMOLOGICAL ARGUMENT FROM CONTINGENCY

Craig, William Lane. *Reasonable Faith.* 3rd ed. Crossway, 2008, chapter 3.

Davis, Stephen T. "The Cosmological Argument and the Epistemic Status of Belief in God." *Philosophia Christi* 1 (1999): 5–15.

———. *God, Reason, and Theistic Proofs*. Reason and Religion. Eerdmans, 1997.

Leibniz, G. W. F. von. "On the Ultimate Origin of Things." In *Leibniz Selections*, 345 55. Edited by P. Wiener. Scribner's, 1951.

———. "The Principles of Nature and of Grace, Based on Reason." In *Leibniz Selections*, 522–33. Edited by P. Wiener. Scribner's, 1951.

O'Connor, Timothy. Theism and Ultimate Explanation: The Necessary Shape of Contingency. Blackwell, 2008.

Pruss, Alexander. "The Leibnizian Cosmological Argument." In *The Blackwell Companion to Natural Theology*, 24–100. Edited by William Lane Craig and J. P. Moreland. Wiley-Blackwell, 2009.

———. *The Principle of Sufficient Reason: A Reassessment*. Cambridge Studies in Philosophy. Cambridge University Press, 2006.

THE *KALAM* COSMOLOGICAL ARGUMENT

Al-Ghāzalī. *Tahafut al-Falasifah* [*Incoherence of the Philosophers*]. Translated by Sabih Ahmad Kamali. Pakistan Philosophical Congress, 1958.

Craig, William Lane. *The Kalam Cosmological Argument*. Repr., Wipf & Stock, 2001.

———. *Reasonable Faith*. 3rd ed. Crossway, 2008, chapter 3.

Craig, William Lane, and Antony Flew. *Does God Exist?* Edited by Stan Wallace. With responses by K. Yandell, P. Moser, D. Geivett, M. Martin, D. Yandell, W. Rowe, K. Parsons, and William Wainwright. Ashgate, 2003.

Craig, William Lane, and James Sinclair. "The *Kalam* Cosmological Argument." In *The Blackwell Companion to*

Natural Theology, 101–201. Edited by William Lane Craig and J. P. Moreland. Wiley-Blackwell, 2009.

Craig, William Lane, and Walter Sinnott-Armstrong. *God? A Debate between a Christian and an Atheist.* Oxford University Press, 2003.

Nowacki, Mark. *The Kalam Cosmological Argument for God.* Studies in Analytic Philosophy. Prometheus, 2007.

Oderberg, David. "Traversal of the Infinite, the 'Big Bang,' and the *Kalam* Cosmological Argument." *Philosophia Christi* 4 (2002): 303–34.

THE TELEOLOGICAL ARGUMENT

Collins, Robin. "A Scientific Argument for the Existence of God: The Fine-Tuning Design Argument." In *Reason for the Hope Within*, 47–75. Edited by Michael J. Murray. Eerdmans, 1999.

———. "The *Teleological* Argument." In *The Blackwell Companion to Natural Theology*, 202–81. Edited by William Lane Craig and J. P. Moreland. Wiley-Blackwell, 2009.

Craig, William Lane. *Reasonable Faith*. 3rd ed. Crossway, 2008, chapter 4.

———. "Richard Dawkins on Arguments for God." In *God Is Great, God Is Good*, 13–31. Edited by William Lane Craig and Chad Meister. IVP, 2009.

Craig, William Lane, and Antony Flew. *Does God Exist?* Edited by Stan Wallace. With responses by K. Yandell, P. Moser, D. Geivett, M. Martin, D. Yandell, W. Rowe, K. Parsons, and William Wainwright. Ashgate, 2003.

Craig, William Lane, and Walter Sinnott-Armstrong. *God? A Debate between a Christian and an Atheist.* Oxford University Press, 2003.

Leslie, John. *Universes.* Routledge, 1989.

Rees, Martin. *Just Six Numbers.* Basic, 2000.

Penrose, Roger. *The Road to Reality.* Knopf, 2005.

Vilenkin, Alex. *Many Worlds in One: The Search for Other Universes.* Hill and Wang, 2006.

THE MORAL ARGUMENT

Alston, William. "What Euthyphro Should Have Said." In *Philosophy of Religion: A Reader and Guide,* 283–98. Edited by William Lane Craig. Rutgers University Press, 2002.

Copan, Paul. "God, Naturalism, and the Foundations of Morality." In *The Future of Atheism: Alister McGrath and Daniel Dennett in Dialogue,* 141-61. Edited by R. Stewart. Fortress, 2008.

Craig, William Lane. *Reasonable Faith.* 3rd ed. Crossway, 2008, chapter 3.

———. "Richard Dawkins on Arguments for God." In *God Is Great, God Is Good,* 13–31. Edited by William Lane Craig and Chad Meister. IVP, 2009.

Craig, William Lane, and Antony Flew. *Does God Exist?* Edited by Stan Wallace. With responses by K. Yandell, P. Moser, D. Geivett, M. Martin, D. Yandell, W. Rowe, K. Parsons, and William Wainwright. Ashgate, 2003.

Craig, William Lane, and Paul Kurtz. *Is Goodness without God Good Enough?* Edited by Nathan King and Robert Garcia. With responses by Louise Antony, Walter Sinnott-Armstrong, John Hare, Donald Hubin, Stephen Layman, Mark Murphy, and Richard Swinburne. Rowman & Littlefield, 2008.

Craig, William Lane, and Walter Sinnott-Armstrong. *God? A Debate between a Christian and an Atheist.* Oxford University Press, 2003.

Linville, Mark. "The Moral Argument." In *The Blackwell Companion to Natural Theology,* 391–448. Edited by William Lane Craig and J. P. Moreland. Wiley-Blackwell, 2009.

Quinn, Philip L. *Divine Commands and Moral Requirements.* Clarendon, 1978.

Ruse, Michael. "Evolutionary Theory and Christian Ethics." In *The Darwinian Paradigm,* 262–69. Routledge, 1989.

Sorley, William R. *Moral Values and the Idea of God.* Macmillan, 1930.

THE ONTOLOGICAL ARGUMENT

Craig, William Lane. *Reasonable Faith.* 3rd ed. Crossway, 2008, chapter 3.

———. "The Ontological Argument." In *To Everyone an Answer,* 124–57. Edited by Francis Beckwith, William Lane Craig, and J. P. Moreland. IVP, 2004.

Davis, Stephen T. *God, Reason, and Theistic Proofs.* Reason and Religion. Grand Rapids: Eerdmans, 1997.

———. "The Ontological Argument." In *The Rationality of Theism,* 93–111. Edited by Paul Copan and Paul K. Moser. Routledge, 2003.

Hick, John H. and Arthur C. McGill. *The Many-faced Argument.* Macmillan, 1967.

Leftow, Brian. "The Ontological Argument." In *The Oxford Handbook for Philosophy of Religion,* 80–115. Edited by William J. Wainwright. Oxford University Press, 2005.

Maydole, Robert. "A Modal Model for Proving the Existence of God." *American Philosophical Quarterly* 17 (1980): 135–42.

——. "The Ontological Argument." In *The Blackwell Companion to Natural Theology,* 553–92. Edited by William Lane Craig and J. P. Moreland. Wiley-Blackwell, 2009.

Plantinga, Alvin. *The Nature of Necessity*. Clarendon, 1974.

Plantinga, Alvin, ed. *The Ontological Argument*. Doubleday, 1965.

Notes

1. "Modernizing the Case for God," *Time* (April 7, 1980), 65–66.
2. That the revolution is ongoing is evident from the appearance last year of *The Blackwell Companion to Natural Theology*, ed. William Lane Craig and J. P. Moreland (Wiley-Blackwell, 2009), a compendious volume of scholarly articles written in defense of a wide variety of theistic arguments.
3. Richard Dawkins, *The God Delusion* (Houghton-Mifflin, 2006).
4. Alexander Pruss, *The Principle of Sufficient Reason: A Reassessment*, Cambridge Studies in Philosophy (Cambridge University Press, 2006); Timothy O'Connor, *Theism and Ultimate Explanation: The Necessary Shape of Contingency* (Blackwell, 2008); Stephen T. Davis, *God, Reason, and Theistic Proofs*, Reason and Religion (Eerdmans, 1997); Robert Koons, "A New Look at the Cosmological Argument," *American Philosophical Quarterly* 34 (1997):

193–211; Richard Swinburne, *The Existence of God,* 2nd ed. (Clarendon, 2004).

5. "In the Beginning: In Conversation with Paul Davies and Philip Adams" (January 17, 2002), http://www.abc.net.au/science/bigquestions /s460625.htm.

6. Alex Vilenkin, *Many Worlds in One: The Search for Other Universes* (Hill and Wang, 2006), 176.

7. Daniel Dennett, *Breaking the Spell: Religion as a Natural Phenomenon* (Viking, 2006), 244.

8. For a discussion of the possibility of atemporal personhood, see my *Time and Eternity: Exploring God's Relationship to Time* (Crossway, 2001), 77–113.

9. Such an exercise of causal power plausibly brings God into time at the very moment of creation.

10. Stuart Hackett, *The Resurrection of Theism: Prolegomena to Christian Apology,* 2nd ed. (Baker, 1982); David Oderberg, "Traversal of the Infinite, the 'Big Bang,' and the *Kalam* Cosmological Argument," *Philosophia Christi* 4 (2002): 303–34; Mark Nowacki, *The Kalam Cosmological Argument for God,* Studies in Analytic Philosophy (Prometheus, 2007); William Lane Craig and James Sinclair, "The *Kalam* Cosmological Argument," in *The Blackwell Companion to Natural Theology,* ed. William Lane Craig and J. P. Moreland (Wiley-Blackwell, 2009), 101–201.

11. Dawkins, *God Delusion,* 77.

12. The argument's proponent doesn't arbitrarily conjure up a terminator to the infinite regress and give it a name. Rather, as we have seen, he presents philosophical and scientific arguments that the regress must terminate in a first member, arguments that Dawkins doesn't discuss. Dawkins himself recognizes that many regresses cannot be infinitely extended (*God Delusion*, 78), but he insists it is by no means clear that God constitutes a natural terminator to the regress of causes. But proponents of the *kalam* argument provide justification for what properties such a terminator must possess, and no name need be given to the first cause: it is simply the personal creator of the universe.

13. We needn't be worried by Dawkins's little argument that omniscience and omnipotence are logically incompatible (*God Delusion*, 78). The impossible task Dawkins envisions for God is just a replay of the old chestnut, "Can God make a rock too heavy for him to lift?" The fallacy of such puzzles is that the task described is logically impossible, and omnipotence doesn't mean the ability to bring about the logically impossible.

14. Dawkins, *God Delusion*, 78.

15. Robert Adams, *Finite and Infinite Goods* (Oxford University Press, 2000); William Alston, "What Euthyphro Should Have Said," in *Philosophy of Religion: A Reader and Guide*, ed. William Lane

Craig (Rutgers University Press, 2002), 283–98; Mark Linville, "The Moral Argument," in *Blackwell Companion to Natural Theology,* ed. William Lane Craig and J. P. Moreland (Blackwell, 2009), 391–448; Paul Copan, "God, Naturalism, and the Foundations of Morality," in *The Future of Atheism: Alister McGrath and Daniel Dennett in Dialogue,* ed. R. Stewart (Fortress, 2008), 141–61; John Hare, "Is Moral Goodness without Belief in God Rationally Stable?" in *Is Goodness without God Good Enough? A Debate on Faith, Secularism, and Ethics,* ed. Nathan King and Robert Garcia (Rowman & Littlefield, 2008); C. Stephen Evans, *Kierkegaard's Ethic of Love: Divine Commands and Moral Obligations* (Oxford University Press, 2004).

16. Cited in Lewis Wolpert, *Six Impossible Things before Breakfast: The Evolutionary Origins of Belief* (Norton, 2006), 215. Unfortunately, Wolpert's reference is mistaken. The quotation seems to be a pastiche from Richard Dawkins, *River out of Eden: A Darwinian View of Life* (Basic, 1996), 133, and Richard Dawkins, "The Ultraviolet Garden," Lecture 4 of 7, Royal Institution Christmas Lectures (1992), https://www.rigb.org/christmas-lectures /watch/1991/growing-up-in-the-universe /ultraviolet-garden.

17. Dawkins, *God Delusion,* 215.

18. Dawkins, *God Delusion,* 221.

19. Dawkins, *God Delusion*, 251.

20. Dawkins, *God Delusion.*, 23, 264, 313–17, 326, 328, 330.

21. Dawkins, *God Delusion*, 78–9.

22. You might think that if the constants and quantities had assumed different values, then other forms of life might well have evolved. But this is not the case. By "life" scientists mean that property of organisms to take in food, extract energy from it, grow, adapt to their environment, and repro-duce. The point is that in order for the universe to permit life so-defined, whatever form organisms might take, the constants and quantities have to be incomprehensibly fine-tuned. In the absence of fine-tuning, not even atomic matter or chemis-try would exist, not to speak of planets where life might evolve!

23. Roger Penrose, "Time-Asymmetry and Quantum Gravity," in *Quantum Gravity* 2, ed. C. J. Isham, R. Penrose, and D. W. Sciama (Clarendon, 1981), 249.

24. Dawkins, *God Delusion*, 144.

25. Dawkins, *God Delusion*, 145.

26. Dawkins, *God Delusion*, 147.

27. Dawkins, *God Delusion*, 145.

28. Stephen Hawking and Roger Penrose, *The Nature of Space and Time*, Isaac Newton Institute Series of Lectures (Princeton University Press, 1996), 20.

29. See http://map.gsfc.nasa.gov/m_mm/mr_limits .html.

30. Duane Dicus, et al., "Effects of Proton Decay on the Cosmological Future," *Astrophysical Journal* 252 (1982): 1, 8.

31. Igor D. Novikov and Yakov B. Zel'dovich, "Physical Processes near Cosmological Singularities," *Annual Review of Astronomy and Astrophysics* 11 (1973): 401–2.

32. Joseph Silk, *The Big Bang,* 2nd ed. (Freeman, 1989), 311–12.

33. Christopher Isham, "Creation of the Universe as a Quantum Process," in *Physics, Philosophy and Theology: A Common Quest for Understanding,* ed. R. J. Russell, W. R. Stoeger, and G. V. Coyne (Vatican Observatory, 1988), 378. Isham's mentioning "continuous creation" is a reference to the defunct Steady State theory.

34. Dawkins, *God Delusion*, 146.

35. For a first-hand account see John Preskill's website: http://www.theory.caltech.edu/~preskill /jp_24jul04.html.

36. S. W. Hawking, "Information Loss in Black Holes," (September 15, 2005): 4, http://arxiv.org/abs /hep-th/0507171.

37. See Roger Penrose, *The Road to Reality* (Knopf, 2005), 762–65.

38. Dawkins, *God Delusion*, 157–58.

39. Dawkins, *God Delusion*, 158.

40. Dawkins, *God Delusion*.

41. See his comments on Keith Ward in *God Delusion*, 150. Ward thinks that the hypothesis of a single cosmic designer is simple, even though he rejects the notion that God is simple in the sense that he doesn't have distinct properties.

42. Dawkins, *God Delusion*, 149.

43. Dawkins, *God Delusion*, 153. God's simplicity has even been construed to mean that he lacks distinct properties, a most implausible doctrine. But the simplicity of an immaterial entity need not imply that that entity lacks distinct properties, like immateriality and self-consciousness.

44. Robin Collins, *The Well-Tempered Universe: God, Fine-Tuning, and the Laws of Nature* (forthcoming); John Leslie, *Universes* (Routledge, 1989); Paul Davies, *Cosmic Jackpot* (Houghton Mifflin, 2007); William Dembski, *The Design Revolution* (IVP, 2004); Michael Denton, *Nature's Destiny: How the Laws of Biology Reveal Purpose in the Universe* (Free Press, 1998); Michael Behe, *The Edge of Evolution: The Search for the Limits of Darwinism* (Free Press, 2007).

45. Alvin Plantinga, *The Nature of Necessity* (Clarendon, 1974); Robert Maydole, "A Modal Model for Proving the Existence of God," *American Philosophical Quarterly* 17 (1980): 135–42; Brian Leftow,

"The Ontological Argument," in *The Oxford Handbook for Philosophy of Religion*, ed. William J. Wainwright (Oxford University Press, 2005), 80–115.

46. Dawkins, *God Delusion*, 83.

47. Dawkins, *God Delusion*, 84.

48. I discuss all five arguments in greater depth in my *Reasonable Faith*, 3rd ed. (Crossway, 2008).